THOUGHT CATALOG BOOKS

This Is Why I'm Guarded

This Is Why I'm Guarded

The Guarded Girl's Guide To Love

NICOLE TARKOFF

THOUGHT CATALOG BOOKS

Brooklyn, NY

Contents

1

This Is Why I'm Guarded

There's a reason why my walls are built so high, and there's a reason it will take you longer than expected to bring them down. There's a reason why I'm guarded.

I'm guarded because I've been hurt before. We all have. My weakness is that I carry the pain with me as a constant reminder that it could happen again. And while this is such a cautious way to walk through life, while instead I could be wildly sprinting, the wild sprint has made me fall and trip before, and the scrapes and burns were painful. So painful that it takes a while to try and run that fast again. So I walk, and I walk carefully noticing my surroundings because I worry if I were to ever fall that hard again, I might not be able to get back up.

I'm guarded because I'm scared of what you'll think, but not scared enough to admit it. I fear your disapproval like a little girl fears the monster under her bed, and right now I will just keep quiet to avoid any disturbance.

I'm guarded because no one has ever protected me as well as I protect myself. My own armor has been stronger than yours, or his, or hers, and it will continue to be until someone shows me otherwise.

I'm guarded because I'm no stranger to failure, and while it has made me stronger, it has also made me more aware of all that can go wrong.

I'm guarded because I've mistakenly invested my trust in those who took it for granted, and because of their disregard, I no longer hand that trust out so easily.

I'm guarded because I see the damage coming before it even happens, and I know that the lucky ones will tell me how unreasonable, pessimistic, and sad this all sounds, but even when you try to tell yourself that this time is different, the reminder seeps back in.

Life will bring hurt and pain, and people will disappoint you, but no one has the ability to break down your walls except for you. I'm guarded because I've chosen to be that way.

2

This Is The Difference Between The Idea You Have Of Him, And Who He Turned Out To Be

You have an idea of what kind of person you want to be with, so you trick yourself into thinking he fits that mold. You need a piece with one round edge, but he has too many corners. So you try to fit him in, and you reposition him in every which way, but you can't change his corners you can only change how you see them.

So you do just that.

You ignore the things you'd rather not acknowledge, and you fall in love with only this part of him, the part that you've created in your mind, and the part that you've fooled yourself into thinking he truly is. And eventually you fool yourself so well that you can't even remember the parts of him you've ignored.

Sometimes it feels so good to be with someone, the person you're with may as well be anyone. But sometimes being alone is the time you figure out most about yourself, about the type of person you are and the type of person you hope to be, and then you'll see that the person you one day *do* love will feel lucky to be with you.

And in the time that you're alone, you'll miss the person you thought you had, but as more time passes you'll realize it wasn't him you loved, it was the idea of him.

Because everyone wants to love someone who loves them back just as much, but most times it's never a balanced scale. One end of the scale usually tips higher than the other, and just when you think it's balancing out, the difference between both ends becomes that much more apparent. And it's good to be a little unbalanced, but when you're at the lower end of the scale, it doesn't feel as good as they say it should. And this is when you start to ignore the voice in your head telling you this isn't right, that he's not right for you, and you're not right for him.

Because you'd rather be with someone wrong for you than be with nobody at all.

But you won't admit it, and that's how you trick yourself into thinking you're perfect for each other. And as you deny your fear of being alone it will eventually catch up to you. Because he might be the one to uncover that fear first, no matter how well you hide it, and if he sees you're scared to be alone even when you're with him, he'll realize it's not him you want to be with, it's who you wish he was.

And then when he leaves you for exactly that reason you won't understand why.

You'll think it's something you did, something you said, and he'll give you reasons that attempt to ease the pain, and you'll continue to wonder what you did wrong. But it was less of what you did and more of how you felt, and how those feelings affected your actions, and how you didn't even realize, were you in love with him, or was it only the idea of him you loved? And when you can answer that question you'll finally start to heal.

3

For All The Girls Who Wonder What Could've Been

When you find yourself alone and thinking about the past, about why he left you, why he hurt you, or what changed that caused things to end, don't ask yourself what could've been, think about what *is*, and what could be.

Don't question whether the wrong person was right for you, whether you made a mistake and so did he, believe that if he wanted to be in your life, he would be. Don't look back and see everything that you lost. Instead think of everything that you gained. Think of what the past has taught you and use it to move forward. Use it to let go.

When you find yourself in a room full of people, family, friends, don't think about how different it would be if he was with you, love the people you surround yourself with, and realize that these are the people who matter. And then realize that he doesn't.

Don't think about what he's doing at this moment when you're apart. Think about how you're strong enough to be without him. Think about how you're finally freed from the grip that held you back, and do not let his absence hold you back even further. Allow his absence to provoke everything in you that will help you to begin again. Allow it to initiate something new, not necessarily with *someone*, but with yourself. Learn things about yourself that you never thought you could. Explore, and be present when you do.

Don't continue to think of what could've been because you'll postpone the ability to be happy with yourself. Remember what happiness was like before him, because you *have* experienced happiness when he wasn't there, and you can continue to experience it now that he's gone. Remember that you were someone before you met him, and realize that you've grown into the person you are now.

Remember who you are. Remember who you want to be. And when you are finally able to remember who that person is, share it with the world, share it with someone who won't make you wonder what could've been, but will make you content with what is.

4

To Every Girl Who Is Tired Of Being Told 'I'm Not Looking For Something Serious'

I know that you feel like you're not good enough. Not good enough for someone to commit to you fully, to commit to you *only*. Not good enough to receive the same love your heart is capable of giving, not good enough to receive any love at all. You feel this way because he told you he wasn't looking for something serious.

So what was he looking for? What did he think *you* were looking for?

Did he think you'd smile and nod your head? 'It's OK to fuck me and never talk to me again.'

Did he think you'd politely go along? 'I'm not looking for anything serious, either.'

Did you think you could change his mind? *You couldn't.*

You never wanted to love someone who didn't love you back, but unrequited love is often the kind that teaches us the most about ourselves, because the love that he doesn't give you, you have to give back to yourself.

You can sit and wonder *why*. Wonder what you don't have that meets the criteria for 'serious.' If you're not something serious, what are you? A mere moment in his timeline? Another face he'll remember but name he'll forget? 'What am I?' you wonder. 'Hopeless,' you respond.

You can sit and wonder *when*. When *will* he be looking for something serious? How long will you have to wait or are you waiting for nothing?

You can sit and wonder *who*. Who will make him want something serious? Will it be you?

When he tells you this don't wonder. Don't ask why, when, or who. Instead have the confidence to understand what it is *you* want. Not from him, but from life, from love, from this constantly changing universe you find yourself in. Have the invincibility to realize that there's something more important than being his 'something serious.' Have the strength to be yourself, and to never change for someone else. Don't try to be his 'something' because who you already are is so much more than that.

I'm not looking for something serious translates to I will never love you the way you wish to be loved, and he didn't. But just because he wasn't looking for something serious, doesn't mean you won't find someone who is. And it sure as hell doesn't mean you don't *deserve* someone who is.

You won't mean *something* to *someone*, you will mean *every-thing* to one person. You'll find them, and they won't tell you they're not looking for something serious. They'll tell you that they've been looking for someone like you for a very long time. And you will feel the same exact way. You will feel loved like you deserve to feel loved.

5

Maybe It's Too Soon To Say I Love You

It's too soon to say I love you because love is just a feeling, and it's something we think that time will confirm, but sometimes we don't recognize that it's real until it's over. We don't need time to confirm our feelings, because while we may not know exactly what love *is*, we know how it *feels*, and we can't help how quickly we feel it.

It's too soon to say I love you because we're terrified of unreciprocated feelings, and the only way we'll know this love is mutual is if one of us takes the chance to say it first. But we're both not sure if loss is worth the risk. And a huge part of love is not allowing the fear of losing someone to keep you from loving them at all. Love is when you're well aware that a person could completely break you, and you continue to take a chance on them regardless.

It's too soon to say I love you because we've both been hurt before. And this time we're reluctant to reveal ourselves so easily because the feeling is familiar, and the last time we felt it, it turned out to be temporary. But not all love will last forever, and the love that doesn't, continues to make us stronger because we constantly look back and learn that the moment we thought we'd never love again, we somehow did.

It's too soon to say I love you because we're living someone else's timeline. We have an idea of how long it's "supposed" to take to know if you truly love someone, and anything sooner is simple infatuation. It's early enough for this to be lust not love, and we each will wait until we recognize the difference, but the moment we stop thinking about when certain things are "supposed" to happen is the moment we truly begin to live.

It's too soon to say I love you, but when we both feel an absence in the quiet, we can't think of anything else to fill it with. And while we both may be thinking it, our thoughts aren't loud enough for either one of us to hear.

It's too soon to say I love you, and everyone else might think we're crazy for wanting to, but it's more bizarre to let others dictate our feelings than it is to just admit to them.

It's too soon to say I love you, but I can't help that every time we say goodbye I want to.

6

I'm Over It, But I Still Think About You

I'm over it, but I still think about you. And at least I'm willing to admit it.

I think about the way you broke my heart, and how long it took me to piece it back together. I think about the promises you made about our future, and how disappointed I was when you broke them. I think about the red flags I should've seen but chose to ignore with hopes that you were right for me, that the warning signs weren't warning signs at all, but just me being scared, scared of love, of everything we could be, of everything you could mean to me, of everything we could mean to *each other*.

Boy, was I wrong. I should've trusted myself, trusted my instincts, because the warning signs were my head telling my heart that it was only a matter of time before you hurt me. And my head was right, and my heart was wrong.

Because my heart wanted to believe that the lies you fed me were true. They tasted so good against my lips and they tasted even better on the way down. And sooner or later those lies became my reality. And I had to live with the fact that someone I thought who cared about me, someone I thought who trusted me, potentially loved me, didn't.

And it hurt like hell, and it took time for me to fully digest what exactly happened. Because you came into my life as quickly as you left it, and you stirred my life around and I began to change direction.

And when you disappeared, the pieces of yourself you left behind still lingered, and I hated that. In fact, they still linger, and I try to ignore them. I try to ignore the fact that when I walk past the place where you first kissed me, I immediately think of you. I try to ignore the fact that I saved one photo of you that I can't seem to delete, and I tell myself it's simply to serve as proof that you even exist, that we once meant something to each other, even though I know it's because I *want* to remember you.

I want to remember the terrible way you made me feel, I want to remember that I never deserve to feel like that again. I'm over it, and I still think of you, but it's because I finally understand that who you are now and who you once were to me, don't matter, but the way you hurt me will serve as a constant reminder of the love that I deserve, the love that you never showed me, the love that someone else will.

7

8 Ways The Girl Whose Heart Has Been Broken Loves Differently

1. She remembers her past as a reminder to not make the same mistakes twice.

Her heart has more cracks and scars than she would like it to, and while the scars serve as constant reminders of heartbreak, they also serve as constant reminders of what went wrong and why. While she can't control whether or not her heart will be broken again, she can control the mistakes she was responsible for, and she can control her ability to never make those same mistakes twice. Girls who have been heartbroken won't love you the same way they loved before, because although they've experienced love that didn't last, they still want to find a love that will.

2. She appreciates what she has when she has it.

When she experiences love again, she's well aware that it can be taken away at any moment, but she appreciates it for what it is every single day. She cherishes the moments you make her feel loved because she knows how it feels when those moments stop.

3. She takes a while to open up emotionally, but when she does, you know it's real.

You might be on the surface with a girl who's been heartbroken for quite some time, and when you try to delve deeper she knows exactly what you're doing. She's apprehensive to trust you with her feelings but when she does, you'll love her even more. Her broken heart hasn't made her numb, it's made her careful. She still feels love, she just needs time to express it, so be patient.

4. She's scared you're going to leave.

It's not surprising that the girl whose heart has been broken worries it will happen again, but the right person will make her feel a happiness that overcomes her fear of loving and being left. It's only a matter of time before she meets the person who makes love a little less scary.

5. She's not afraid to leave if she's unhappy.

She's familiar with unhappiness, and it's not a feeling she finds favorable, especially in relationships. Her fear of being left is as strong as her capability to leave when she wants to. Her broken heart has helped her realize the love that she deserves, and she's not afraid to leave the wrong person to find it.

6. She knows herself pretty well.

Her broken heart has allowed her to look at her life when she feels like it's falling apart, and it has also allowed her to recognize what she needs to do to rebuild it. She knows what makes her happy, and what makes her want to crawl into a corner and cry, she knows what she needs to feel a little more like herself.

7. She's able to survive on her own, so if you're in her life, she wants you there.

Chances are she's not the only one to blame for her broken heart, but in the after math the only option she had was to be alone, and while she may seek temporary companionship with everyone who's wrong for her, she knows that being alone doesn't have to be *lonely*. Loneliness is something she's learned to not be afraid of, and she's perfectly capable of living life without the comfort of companionship.

8. She will make sure you feel loved.

She knows how it feels to receive a love that's less than she deserves, so she will do everything she can to make sure you never have to feel that way. A broken heart doesn't mean she's incapable of love, it means she wants to give her heart to someone who will take care of it. She has plenty of love to give, she just hasn't found the person who will receive it, and give the same amount back.

8

Find Someone Who Makes You Unafraid To Love

Love can be as terrifying as it is exciting, but the fear of love shouldn't keep you from feeling it. No matter how badly you were hurt the first time, or the second, your broken heart will begin to heal when you find the courage to love again. And you *will* love again, because even if you don't want to, even if you tell yourself love is hopeless, or temporary, or just an emotion people believe in to simply survive, one day you'll find a person who will make you realize it's real.

That love, even if it's not forever, exists.

Find someone who makes you hopeful instead of fearful. Someone who holds your hand like they never want to let it go. Someone whose touch makes you feel trust. Someone whose presence makes you feel comfort. Someone who gives you hope that love can be authentic, because they make you feel a love that is.

Find someone who shares their life, rather than rearranges it to make you fit. Someone who *has* a place for you, not someone who *makes* a place for you. Someone who doesn't need to make you *feel* like you belong because you know that you do.

Find someone who loves you for every right reason. Someone who can't stand to see you sad. Someone who enjoys your happiness, someone who wants the best for you as much as they want it for themselves.

Find someone who makes you feel lucky. Lucky that they chose and continue to choose you. Find someone who feels as lucky to be with you as you feel to be with them.

Find someone who appreciates your success, someone who makes you *want* success. Not to competitively be better than they are, but because you want to be the best version of yourself when you're with them.

Find someone who challenges you. Someone who won't always agree with your thoughts or your opinions, but will hear them, listen to them, and react with honesty. And not always honesty that is kind, but honesty that you'll appreciate because it comes from a place of love, not envy.

Find someone who makes you a little less terrified of love. Someone who makes the excitement of love overcome the fear of it.

<u>9</u>

I Hope You Found What You're Looking For

I hope you're happy now, but I hope this not out of spite or passive aggressive ill will. I hope you're happy because it has finally become apparent to me how well-hidden real happiness can be, and how much searching you have left to find it.

It's like when you're looking for that one thing that you've misplaced, and you spend hours on end rummaging through your space just to find it, and by the time you're done looking it looks like the earth turned upside down, and you've found everything it is that you weren't originally looking for. And then one day, when you're not looking, when you're not relentlessly searching from top to bottom, that one thing you've been looking for the entire time mysteriously appears.

When you were with me, I was the one thing you found that you weren't originally looking for.

And when you found me, it was a nice surprise, but I wasn't *it*. I wasn't that one thing you turned your world upside-down for, I was just something you found along the way. And I always felt like something was missing, and now I realize it's because every moment we were together, you were looking for something else.

I couldn't make you happy, not because I didn't have enough love to give, or because I was in someway insufficiently unworthy, but because I wasn't right for you. Because we weren't right for each other. But at that time I thought we were. I thought I was that *one* thing you were looking for, and that's why it hurt so bad when you left.

That's why I woke up the next morning with my eyes swollen shut, I've never been a pretty cryer. And that's why after an entire week of tears I became angry. Because the sadness can only last so long.

And after the pain of your departure hit me, I began to resent you.

I resented the way I thought you mislead me, and I resented the way I felt like maybe it was me who misunderstood your promises. Maybe it was me who expected too much. Maybe it was my fault for not seeing that I wasn't what you set out to find.

But now that time has passed I realize it was not your fault or mine for a love that never grew. There's not necessarily always one person at fault for a heart that's been hurt.

Because it seems that the victim is always the person who was left, and never the one who leaves, but I think all along your heart was much more damaged than mine.

And I think the damage that your heart has clearly suffered prevents you from finding that one thing you're looking for, because I don't think you even know what that one thing is. I don't think you'd recognize it even if you found it.

And as you continue to turn your world upside down in search of this special *something*, I can only hope that there are fewer hearts in the path of your destruction. I hope you've found what you're looking for so that you can stop hurting everyone else along the way. And I hope that if you hurt her next, she makes the same realization I do. I hope she realizes that it's not her heart that needs healing, it's yours.

10

Some Love Is Worth Remembering

Sometimes the love you lose makes you understand its existence because you realize it wasn't love that you lost, it was a person. And maybe what we fail to understand is how love can never really be lost, and even when we think it is, we can remember it, and we can go back to it in our minds and think about how we felt when that love was more than just a memory.

And even if it is only in our thoughts, that love can be relived for just a moment. And while it may not be reality, it is the only thing we have to hold onto. Because some love is harder to let go of. Some love we may not even realize we carry with us. We feel the weight of it, but we can't see it, and it attempts to hold us back when all we want to do is move forward. But maybe that love has to be able to move forward *with* us.

Some love is worth remembering because of how it made us feel, because of how it built us and broke us, and how all of that destruction made us learn something about ourselves. And it's fascinating to see how we continued to live after we *thought* that love was gone.

But we *thought* wrong because we shouldn't look at love as something that can be lost and found, but as a feeling that makes us feel alive when we have it. When we think love is lost we can only hope that we will find it again. And sometimes we go searching for love but instead we find ourselves.

In a way, losing makes us stronger because we have to learn to live without everything that has been lost. And we can't magically erase the time when it was there, and we shouldn't want to. Because your life isn't a dry erase board, it's a concrete sidewalk, and the cement is constantly wet, and people will walk through it and their footprints will remain. And every impression is a memory, and some of those memories are harder to look back on, but usually the ones we hate to remember are the ones that taught us the most valuable lesson.

And that's the type of love and loss that makes us grow, that shapes us into the people we become. And maybe it is childish to think that everything happens for a reason, or if not childish, impractical, but when you think about it, nothing about love is practical.

We're all looking for answers that may not exist, and maybe that's why people tell us it's best to let go, but I don't think it's harmful to remember the *feelings* you were holding onto, I think it's harmful to hold onto the person. Because while holding onto a person can cause damage, remembering the way that person made you feel can serve as a reminder that you're capable of feeling at all. We're not numb to love, we're scared to experience it again.

11

7 Signs You're Running From Your Feelings Because You've Been Hurt Before

1. You rarely ever openly admit you 'like' someone.

When your best friend asks how you feel about him, you'll say you're on the fence. The moment you admit you like him, is the moment you think everything will fall apart. Don't be afraid to like someone just because you're scared it will end the way your last relationship did.

2. When you do really like someone, you look for something to be wrong with them.

If you can't see any red flags, don't go looking for them because chances are they're a figment of your imagination. You will know when something is off, and if you recognize it then it's fine to run in the other direction, but if you're only seeking what is wrong because you're scared he could be right for you, you're avoiding the way you really feel.

3. You tell people you're not looking for a relationship.

Especially the people you're dating. Before they even begin to think about having a relationship with you, you make it a point to tell them that is NOT what you want. You might think you don't *want* a relationship, but when you meet someone that makes you wonder if you do, you might need to adjust your usual mindset. A relationship is half dependent on the other person, and if the feelings are clearly there, then why hide them? When you worry about how the relationship will end it prevents you from ever letting it begin.

4. You casually hook up with people you have no real interest in.

No interest means no attachment. Your casual hook up insures an easily said goodbye. When you begin to have feelings a goodbye begins to feel more like an absence than a simple farewell. You'd rather have unattached sex with someone you're not into, than be left by someone you care about, but what you need to realize is not everyone will leave you.

5. You like to 'keep your options open.'

You keeping your options open is another way of saying you're too scared to settle on one person. It's not because you think you're too good for them, it's because you're scared you'll eventually become unhappy without them.

6. When things don't workout you pretend that you didn't like them anyway.

Don't kid yourself, you were enjoying your time when you were with them, and just because things didn't workout doesn't mean you have to act like you were never interested. What good are you doing yourself or any one else by refusing to acknowledge your true feelings?

7. You're basically allergic to their feelings and emotions.

If someone you're dating ever tells you the extent of their feelings or how much they enjoy being with you, you practically break out in hives. Don't fear communication, there are plenty of people who would kill for their significant other to admit their feelings aloud. They're putting themselves out there when they tell you how they feel, and they trust that you'll listen. You're not allergic to feelings, you're allergic to hearing them.

12

The Difference In Being Left, And Leaving The One You Love

When you're *left* by the one you love, you wonder what you did wrong. You wonder what made them stop loving you, and you wonder if you could've done anything to change it.

When *you're the one leaving*, you hear the thoughts they leave unspoken. You feel like you know exactly what they're thinking and you wish you could stop them from ruminating on these distorted beliefs. You know they're trying to piece together the spaces you left open, but not even you know how to fill in the gaps. You didn't realize leaving would be so difficult.

When you're *left* by the one you love, your hurt manifests itself in different ways. Sometimes the hurt comes out as anger, as spiteful words you use to hurt them back. Sometimes the hurt doesn't come out at all, and lives in deep denial. Sometimes the hurt numbs you to anything else so that hurt is the *only* feeling.

When *you're the one leaving,* hurt causes a different type of pain. You don't feel the force of the initial impact, but you see and feel the bruises that form and remain long after. You feel like the hurt you're feeling is unfair to be felt, but you're hurting because of the hurt you caused in someone else.

When you're *left* by the one you love, you hope time will heal the pain. You count the days, weeks and months that go by and ask yourself if it's actually getting any better. You think it's *time* that's lessening the impact, but really it's just *living*.

When *you're the one leaving*, time is insignificant. You don't feel it passing or standing still, you just sort of know it's happening. You don't stay up at night thinking about tomorrow, you just take it day by day.

When you're *left* by the one you love, you're reminded of them at every corner. They're waiting for you in the restaurant you ate at on your birthday, in the park where you had your first date, they're everywhere. And even when you try to avoid these places, in fear of the memories they'll bring up, there's no running or hiding that will make them go away. Even in your own apartment, you sit on the couch you both had to build together.

When *you're the one leaving*, the memories still follow you around, but the avoiding is less of an undertaking. You don't feel the excessive need to run or hide because that restaurant doesn't scare you, and neither does the park. They make you remember, but you don't mind the memories, you actually enjoy them.

Being *left* and *leaving* are two different things, but it doesn't make either one any less difficult.

13

I Haven't Thought About You In A While

It took a long time for me to leave the thought of you behind. It was an effort, not an occurrence. But I shouldn't have to *try* to forget you, because that means you're still very much remembered.

I remember you because you're gone, and I think of you because of the way you left.

But when I think of you, it doesn't mean I'm holding on; it means I'm retracing my steps. And when I try to fit my feet back in the footprints that I left when I was with you, I can't. Because we're both pointing in different directions. And every time I try to go back I end up in the same place. Here. Because retracing you is like tracing a circle, I'm not sure if I ended where I started, so I'll just keep going, but I can't begin to draw another shape unless I lift the pen.

And each time you cross my mind the doubt crosses with it. What could I have done differently? How could I have convinced you stay? But it wasn't you who needed convincing, it was me, because I hadn't convinced myself that this was something I deserved.

But from every mistake there's a lesson learned, and you have been quite the teacher. Because when I was with you I felt whole, and when you left I felt depleted, but now I realize needing someone else to make you full only leaves you empty.

So now that you're gone I find other ways to fill my time, other thoughts to fill my head. But every once in a while you creep back in. And when that happens I think about how long it's been since I thought of you before, and each time the gap widens. So will there ever come a time when I don't think of you at all?

14

You're Not A Failure At Love Because You're Heartbroken

There's no such thing as failing at love, there's only refusing to try. You fail when you allow fear to keep you comfortable.

Love isn't comfortable, it's scary. It's knowing there is someone out there who makes you feel like your life would fall apart without them, and it's living with the perpetual fear of that possibility.

And when that moment becomes reality you feel like you've been broken. You feel your life move forward, but you're walking through it facing backwards. One foot steps behind the other, instead of in front, and the past is a place you continue to retreat to, but when you lose some *thing* it's completely normal to retrace your steps, and losing some *one* is no different.

One thing that continues to pass is time, and whenever you're in pain you wish it would pass by faster.

And others will tell you that time heals all wounds, but you won't feel yourself recovering until one day you wake up and the scab is completely gone. But you didn't one day suddenly become better, it was a process that you were unaware was happening. Because sometimes you only realize you're healing until after you're healed.

And in the duration of this healing, when time feels slow and every day's a struggle, the only thing to do is cope. So you attempt to distract yourself in every way possible, with people, things, substances, anything that will keep your thoughts from filling the silence. And then you realize that distractions only occupy your mind for so long, and that's when the feeling of failure kicks in.

And failure turns into frustration because even if you succeed at everything else, the one place you want success to happen it won't. But heartbreak isn't failure, it's trial and error. It's a step taken toward something you thought was the right direction, but turned out to be wrong. And most times you don't automatically reroute. You wander and feel lost.

But the time you spent giving your heart to someone who broke it is just as valuable as the time it takes to heal. Because the time you devoted to learning about someone else resulted in you learning about yourself.

It isn't failure if you've become more aware of who you are and what you need; it would be failure to continue to settle for anything less.

And suddenly you find yourself adjusting to a new way of life without the person who used to make you happy, but you shouldn't think of happiness as something that occurred in the past. Happiness is something you need to make room for in your future, and it needs to originate from a source within yourself. Don't attempt to make your life happier by finding someone. Find happiness and then find someone to share it with. And find the strength to risk heartbreak as a result.

Your broken heart is an indication that you have enough courage to give so much of yourself to someone that you get hurt in return. **You're not a failure at love because your heart is broken, you're a failure at love if you let the fear of heartbreak keep you from loving at all.**

15

For The Girls Who Follow Their Heart And Not Their Head

We fall in love easily. We like to think it's because we have a lot of love to give, but maybe it's because we're foolish. Because we lead with our heart and not with our head. Because our mind is capable of seeing everything our hearts are blinded by. Our brain tells us to run away, and our heart tells us to stay.

But what if our foolishness is the same thing that leads us to our happiness? What if we don't want to accept that it could lead us to sadness instead? It's okay to be hopeful, our hope is not stupidity, it is courage. Because it takes strength to listen to your heart with the risk of it being broken, but it is the way others mistake your openness for weakness that leads to hurt and pain. They mistake your vulnerability for desperation. Because if we are vulnerable, honest, or god forbid, express ourselves in a way that corresponds to exactly how we feel, we are too much. We are overdoing it, trying too hard, getting too attached. We are desperate for love. But following your heart doesn't make you desperate for love, it makes you open to finding it.

And we tend to find what we mistakenly think is love over

and over again. Because sometimes our heart is wrong. Sometimes it makes mistakes. But every step our heart navigates, is made for a reason. Our heart tells us where to go only when it feels something. And acknowledging the feeling is better than ignoring it. We follow our hearts with every right intention, but sometimes our right intentions lead to expectations, and then the expectations lead to disappointments.

But real love isn't disappointing. It can be trying and difficult, and complicated, but it isn't full of empty promises; it's full of support, encouragement, and confidence. This is the love our hearts are trying to find, and we follow them in hopes that one day they will find it.

We may fall in love easy, but when we do, we fall hard. And while our mind is more pragmatic, our hearts are drowning in emotions. We want our head to match our heart, but sometimes our hearts are too stubborn to listen.

16

She's Happy Now, He's Still The Same Piece Of Shit

He looked the same. The part in his hair was the same, the scruff on his chin the same, his drink of choice, Jack and Coke, the same. Nothing about his physical appearance was different, and she imagined nothing about his intellect was different either. She assumed he was still the same self-absorbed, ungrateful bastard that he was when they were together.

She assumed he had learned nothing from their relationship, that he was still set on the thought that she should've thanked him for leaving her, that he was doing her a favor, it was for her own good, and now she realizes while at the moment of heartbreak she felt like the world was ending, his leaving was the best thing that could've happened to her.

When she was with him, the convenience of companionship concealed the red flags. She was blinded to the fact that he loved himself more than he loved her, blinded to the fact that his words didn't match his actions. At that time words were enough. She only needed to hear how much she meant to him, and didn't care whether or not he showed it, because being with someone who could proclaim love but not demonstrate it was better than being with nobody at all.

But now she was different. Now she was happy with herself, her life, and she didn't think of companionship in terms of convenience she thought of it in terms of who she wanted to share her life with. She realized companionship was not something you should crave because you're scared of being lonely, but something that depends on the person you're calling your companion. She realized it was only the idea of him she loved.

And her happiness led her to stop trying, not in an 'I give up on love' kind of way, but in a way that she wanted to live her life searching for herself, and maybe someone along the way would make that discovery with her. And someone did.

It wasn't love at first sight. She didn't feel a magic spark when she first shook his hand and told him her name, it was an average introduction that turned into an intoxicated escape. A summer night of drunken kisses in a freezing pool, and innocent fondling on a less than sturdy hammock, but she loved kissing him. She loved his touch against her skin and the way he pushed her hair behind her ear. She loved the way his earring felt cold against her chest as he kissed her neck.

She loved their night together, but never imagined it would turn into something more, that this boy would be the first to tell her 'I love you,' and the first boy she's ever said it back to. She was happy now, happy with herself, and the people she chose to include in her life, she was in love. In love with this boy who *showed* her love and didn't just *say* it. And when she felt love with him she realized that this person from her past sitting across the bar was not someone who mattered, he was the shell of a person she used to know, used to share her life with, and while she wished she had never met him, he lead her to her current happiness.

She hadn't seen him since the breakup, since he asked if they could still be friends and she told him no, since he told her that she wouldn't realize it now, but eventually she'd thank him. And standing in that bar where it felt like two worlds were colliding, where the boy she thought she loved from her past was in the same room as the boy she currently knew she loved in the present, she thought of everything she wanted to say to the one who left her, the one who hurt her.

She was angry, angry that finally when she stopped thinking about him, finally when she was happy with someone else, happy with herself, when he was no longer in her mind, he somehow found a way to pop back in. She hated him for that.

When he left her she repeated over and over the things she would tell him if she ever saw him again. Words filled with fury, sadness, pain, words she didn't know she had in her, but would feel so good to get out. But she hadn't seen him. She hadn't been given the chance to purge her pent up emotions, splatter them across his face to see how he'd react. She never called, she never texted, she let it go, but she waited for the day when she'd run into him, the day she could say the things she felt would give her closure. And it never happened. Until now.

She felt like the universe was trying to tell her something.

That her ex was in this bar with her and the boy she currently loved because the world was trying to show her some type of metaphorical venn diagram. That the universe was telling her to think about the terrible way her ex treated her and how it was *so wrong* compared to the boy who currently treats her *so right*. And she wanted to storm up to him, this ghost from her past and say all the things she felt inside, but she didn't want to hurt the boy who stood beside her. Didn't want him to think she was holding onto something. But she knew he was confident in her love, and she was confident in his. So she did.

She approached her ex who stood across the bar waiting for another whiskey. The walk felt infinitely longer than it should've, and when she finally stood behind him, she downed the remaining tequila soda in her glass, liquid courage. She tapped him on the shoulder expecting him to turn around with shock written across his forehead. When he looked at her she felt a tinge of regret. Regret for walking up to him, regret for ever meeting him, ever dating him, ever sharing a part of her life with him, and before he could even say hello, she said exactly what she wanted to say.

It didn't sound rehearsed, it didn't sound planned, because everything she said came out differently than she ever thought it would. It came out with confidence, with assurance that she was currently in the place she belonged, that her life was finally full of meaning, that she wasn't purging her emotions because she hadn't let him go, but because she needed to release a part of herself she didn't like. This was for her, not him. This was *about* her, not him.

After she flawlessly executed her impromptu soliloquy, she didn't wait for his reply. She put her empty glass on the bar beside him, picked up his Jack and Coke, turned around and walked away. Away to the boy who currently loved her. The boy who showed her what real love is. And when she finally made it back to him he looked at her and smiled and he asked her how she felt. And she told him she was happy.

Imagining all of this, imagining her saying everything she's ever dreamt of saying to her ex, taking his Jack and Coke, walking away without letting him say anything in return, made her realize she didn't need to say anything at all. She didn't need to give him the satisfaction of thinking she still cared, she didn't need to waste her energy on someone who didn't deserve it. She knew he was the same person who left her, the same self-centered bag of shit who hurt her, and that no matter what emotions, words, or thoughts she purged on him, would only give her temporary release.

She saw her ex standing on the other side of the bar, and she looked at the loving boy who stood beside her, she grabbed his hand and said, "Let's get out of here." She walked past her ex and didn't say a word, didn't tap him on the shoulder, or look into his eyes, she left. And she walked out of his life like he walked out of hers, and she was happy.

17

You'll Let Him Go When You Become Your Own Person

What is it that you're holding on to?

Is it the way he said your name when he told you that he loved you, or is it the way he looked at you when he told you good-bye? Is it the way he first met you as if he *had* to have you, had to make you *his*, or is it the way he left you so easily as if you never really mattered?

What is it that you're holding onto that won't allow you to let go?

You can't let go of him just like you can't let go of the person you were when you were with him. But he's gone now, and when he left, he didn't just leave *you*, he left the two of you together, he left the 'us' behind. And the 'us' became *I* for the both of you.

And the *I* that you suddenly, maybe unexpectedly, found yourself with felt incomplete, and that scared you. **Because you felt like you no longer knew yourself. You felt like you no longer knew who you were without him.** And while uncertainty made you feel stuck, made you feel that every choice was the wrong one, you need to realize that you won't be able to tell if you're making the wrong decision until after you've made it.

Don't be afraid to move forward. Don't be afraid to try.

Don't be afraid of who you are without him, and don't hold onto the person you were when you were with him. Because time will pass and new love might not immediately happen, new love *won't* immediately happen. New love will feel like it's everywhere you are not, and no matter how hard you go looking for it, you most likely won't find it. Because when you try to find someone who cares about you in attempt to forget someone who used to, you'll only find people to fill in the gaps. And when the gaps reveal themselves again you'll realize it's you that needs to fill them, not anyone else.

Because you need some time to figure out the 'I' before you find another 'us.' Because the way to move on from how he hurt you isn't to find someone new, it's to become comfortable with yourself. To be able to learn what it is you love, other than a person.

And at first you might feel lonely, or unwanted, maybe even underserving, but as soon as you become less scared of independence you'll begin to understand yourself a little better. You'll begin to become someone else without him. You'll let him go when you become your own person.

18

I Thought You Broke My Heart, But I Found A Way To Fix It

I thought you broke my heart because when our time together ended I didn't want to be alone. The fear I had of being hurt became my reality like I knew it would, and the fear of loneliness came with it. There were promises and plans, but none of that mattered because the moment you *wanted* to leave, you did.

And at first I was completely angry, mad that you would hurt me like you said you never would, frustrated with the words you said, and how your actions did not reflect them. And then the anger I had towards you became doubt I had towards myself. Maybe it was me who wasn't good enough, it was me who didn't deserve your affection, it was my fault you left me, something I *did*, something I *didn't*.

And once I completely absorbed that self-doubt I began to learn what heartbreak feels like. And it's strange that even though you once felt happy before this person came into your life, when they leave, you feel like you'll never be happy again. But happiness is something you find within yourself, it just takes a bit of searching. And when this realization became something I accepted, I began to fix the heart I thought you broke.

When someone breaks your heart you tend to guard it more carefully, but just because one person hurts you, doesn't mean you should convince yourself that everyone else will do the same. When you shield yourself from hurt that hasn't happened yet, you shield yourself from feeling anything at all.

And when I learned to let my guard down, I learned how to let people in. And when you allow someone to learn all of you, you begin to accept the parts of yourself you were reluctant for others to see. And you learn not only to accept yourself, but you also learn that you should only share your life with someone who will do the same, someone who accepts, enjoys, and cherishes every part of you.

So when I thought you broke my heart all of these realizations came to light, and it turns out you didn't break it, you actually made it stronger.

19

Read This When You're Scared Of Being Vulnerable

Sometimes people mistake vulnerability for weakness, because while others build walls up to prevent anyone from coming in, you bring walls down to let yourself be free.

But it takes more strength to free yourself than it does to stay caged in.

And while those who consider themselves strong, or tough, or hard, carry on as though nothing bothers them, as though nothing can break them or make them waver, you wear it on your face that you're no stranger to being broken. And although you let others see the fact that you've been hurt before, you still carry on.

Because you don't let vulnerability defeat you or define you, you let it guide you.

And you're in a place where you're susceptible to be hurt again, because that's the position you put yourself in when you acknowledge that your head and your heart are of equal importance, but the benefit of being vulnerable is that you don't allow the fear of how others will respond to prevent you from showing them a part of who you are.

Vulnerability is such a fragile term, but while those who are vulnerable are easily broken, they are also fearless. Because it takes a tremendous amount of courage to put yourself out there. Vulnerability involves taking chances. It means you're willing to risk destruction for something greater.

You're aware that everything could fall apart, but you do it for love, you do it for life itself, because you'd rather be fragile if *pretending* to be strong means constantly wondering, 'What if?'

But being vulnerable *is* being strong, because if everything does fall apart, you realize there's nothing left to do but clean up and start over. It takes strength to admit you're not indestructible.

Being strong isn't being fear*less*, it's admitting fear's presence and allowing it to push you forward rather than hold you back.

Vulnerability uses fear as fuel because you sacrifice hurt for haven. And in acknowledging your fears you're acknowledging a part of who you are that maybe you're reluctant to express.

Because all the times you wish you could convey the things you're feeling and say the thoughts you're thinking, vulnerability comes in and gives those thoughts the voice they didn't have. Vulnerability is insecurity's microphone.

Vulnerability is accepting the part of yourself that you buried the deepest, and it's an attempt to share that part with someone else. The benefit of being vulnerable is that you finally begin to realize no one expects you to be perfect, and you begin to understand that you don't have to be.

20

Don't Change To Find Love, Let Love Change You

You tell yourself relationships mean compromise, but how long will it take you to realize you're compromising who you are to become what he wants you to be?

To say that you deserve someone who accepts you is common knowledge, but sometimes we're so eager to find love that we get fooled in the process. Because you want love, and while you already know that you deserve it, you think you might need a little work before you find it. So you begin to change.

You begin to change in hopes that he will love you for what you become because you see that he's not loving you for what you currently are. But if you're looking to change, you need to change for *yourself*, and not for anyone else. When you change for someone else you're nurturing the parts of you that you created *for him*, for her, for them. And that's when you begin to lose the parts of yourself you used to love.

Because even if it kills you to admit it, there was a time when you liked yourself, and there were plenty of things you liked *about* yourself, but when you realized that wasn't good enough for him you began to question what about you was truly likable, truly lovable. And because he made you feel unlovable, you tried to become someone he *would* love.

In the beginning it was almost effortless. You became hopeful because he began to like the person you were manifesting, and the happiness you felt when he began to show you love made you oblivious to the fact that you were trying to be someone else, that you were being everyone but yourself.

Because all you ever wanted was his affection, his attention, his touch, his kiss, his admiration. You wanted him to look at you like you were the best thing that's ever happened to him. And while it sounds desperate to desire the attention that someone clearly isn't giving you, it's even more desperate to begin to change yourself in efforts to receive it.

Because you shouldn't have to work for his affection, you shouldn't have to change for him to notice you, appreciate you, you shouldn't have to change for him to *love you*.

Let love change you, don't change to find love.

Because when you find a love that's real it *will* change you. It won't make you a *different* person, it will make you a *better* person. Because the person that you find it with will change *with* you, not *for* you. You'll change *together*.

And you'll want to hold onto this person for dear life, but you won't find them. Because if you want to find a love that changes you, you have to let go of those you changed for in order to find it.

21

For All The Girls Who Think He's Looking For A Reason To Leave

He's not looking for a reason to leave, but if you continue to let your doubt overpower the feelings that you have for him, he just might. Because the scenarios you create in your head, how you imagine him leaving, walking out of your life only to see him years later as a stranger, as a person who *looks* familiar, but doesn't *feel* familiar, have nothing to do with him and everything to do with you.

Because he treats you the way you deserve to be treated, and you've waited so long for that to happen. To find someone who loves you for who you are, who sees your flaws as something to embrace rather than to hide, someone who truly wants the best for you, supports you when you're at your worst, but more importantly at your best, because he loves without envy or jealousy or any other needless behavior that sours your taste of happiness. He brings you happiness rather than depleting the source of it you already have within yourself.

And because he's everything you've ever wanted, you're scared. You're scared that if you haven't already given him a reason to leave he will find one.

And then you begin to convince yourself that he's searching for one, for a reason to leave you, but it's you who's searching. You're looking for the reason as to why he's with you. And when you can't find it, you begin to think of every reason as to why he *shouldn't* be. Why he shouldn't be with you, and why he *should* be with someone else.

Because every insecurity you could ever imagine, his perfection brings it out of you. You think he's too good for you, that he could find someone prettier, funnier, smarter, someone who would give him the world even if it meant giving away herself, but that's what is so beautiful about you. That you've found someone you want to give *everything* to, and you still maintain every part of yourself while doing so. And that's exactly what he loves about you.

You're scared that someone could love you the same way you love them, but he's not waiting for a reason to leave, he's waiting for you to accept that he chooses to stay.

He chooses to love you, and he chooses to have you in his life. Everything he does for you, he chooses to. Because people choose who they love, and he chose you.

<u>22</u>

7 Reasons She's Scared To Open Up To You, And How To Earn Her Trust So That She Will

1. She's scared of pushing you away.

She wish you could hear the thoughts in her head that she's afraid to say aloud, like how she loves you so much it scares her, and how she feels like her life might fall apart without you, but you can't *hear* what's going on inside her head, you can only *see* what's going on outside of it. It's impossible to know that when she grabs your hand after you kiss her cheek she's saying "You're incredible," just like it's impossible to know whether or not she'll say "I love you" in return, but know that she's hesitant because she doesn't want her feelings to scare you as much as they scare her.

2. Her ex broke her heart.

The last time she let her guard down, she was let down in return. Her ex tried relentlessly to open her up, and whether she failed to or finally let him in, the relationship didn't turn out the way she thought it would. It doesn't matter who hurt who or why, what matters is that it's over, and in the past, and she's with you because she's ready to move on and already has. Now you need to be open with her, communicate with honesty, say how you really feel. If you can be honest with her, it will make her feel comfortable enough to be honest with you. If she feels like you have your guard up, she'll build her guard even higher.

3. She thinks the skeletons in her closet are too much for you to handle.

There may be a specific reason she's not opening up, something from her past, a scar she doesn't want you to see because she thinks you'll look at her like she's *damaged*. If you love her you won't judge her by the person she was, you'll see her for the person she now is, and you'll do everything you can to help her become the person she hopes to be. Show her that the past doesn't scare you, that whatever happened in her life before is different now that she has you.

4. She cares about you so much it scares her.

Her closed off tendencies aren't any indication that she doesn't care about you, they're indication that she's scared she cares about you *too much*. Questioning what your life would be like without someone, and not being able to imagine the answer is terrifying. This is what she experiences when she tries to imagine her life without you. Don't let her imagination drift like that. Insure her that you're not going anywhere. Let her know that you appreciate how much she cares about you, let her know that her caring, her feeling, is not something to be afraid of, but something to share because if you feel that deeply about her in return, you're probably just as terrified.

5. She's given her heart to all the wrong people.

Maybe she isn't opening up to you because she has opened up to too many people who didn't appreciate it. They aren't necessarily people who have done her wrong, but they are people who haven't cared about her in the way she wanted them to. She was so eager to give her heart to someone, she gave it to almost anyone, and this doesn't make her desperate or *hopeless*, it makes her *hopeful*. She gave her heart away so easily before, because she hoped that each person she gave it to would feel something in return. And now that her love has been refuted one too many times, she thinks the one person who's not only willing to accept it, but return her love, will refute it again like all of the rest. Demonstrate that her love is not something to refute, but something to cherish.

6. Sometimes she thinks she doesn't deserve you.

She's guarded because her deepest fear is that she doesn't deserve the one person who's willing to show her the kind of love that makes her happy, the kind of love that makes her wonder what she did to deserve someone like you. But you feel the same way about her, and you both need to realize that the beautiful thing about love is how lucky you feel to have found this person. Don't wonder what you did to deserve them, think about how lucky you feel that you chose each other.

7. She's scared that the happiness she feels with you is only temporary.

She fears that the moment she's truly happy is the moment that all of her happiness will disappear. She has to learn that the euphoria she feels with you is partly because you make her happy with herself. When you're with her, really be with her, and allow the happiness she feels in each moment with you to eliminate her worry of the future. Because while you can't guarantee the happiness you experience together will be ever-lasting, you can appreciate every moment you feel that it will be.

23

This Is The Fear Of Loving And Being Left

You've been there before just not in the same way. You're flying when you're with him, and even when he's gone, your feet still don't touch the ground. When you're not thinking about anything, you're thinking about him, and when you're thinking about everything else your somehow reminded of the two of you together, of the happiness you share, and how at this moment he makes you as happy as you make him, and that's all you've ever wanted.

And then you start to wonder what it is about him that you really like, because you have this dark place of doubt that he will leave you, and it's hidden so deep beneath the surface that only you know it's there. And you think you're good at hiding it, but eventually that dark place of doubt that has sunken so deep will begin to float, and soon you won't be the only one who knows it's there.

Because when everything is going well you're waiting for disaster, for something to come in and take it all away. But when you're too worried about what's to come you can't enjoy what is already there. You can't actively try to diminish your fear of loving and being left, you have to accept that people come into your life because you *let* them in, and whether or not they choose to leave is out of your control, but if you shut them out, you'll never know.

And not knowing makes your mind run in circles. One minute you're telling yourself the risk isn't worth it, and the next you're convinced you have nothing to lose. And you'll never really know the right way to go, because if something goes wrong you'll look back and blame the path you chose, but maybe you need to realize you're not as lost as you think you are. Just because you can't see the final destination doesn't mean you're unsure of which direction you want to move. Deep down you know exactly where you want to go, but each step is full of more and more apprehension. And that apprehension will consume the happiness he brings into your life, so don't let it.

You know how you feel about him, and it scares you, but you can't allow the fear of being left to prevent you from moving forward, because if you fear love, you'll never allow yourself to truly find it.

24

7 Fears People Have About Committing And Why The Right Person Will Make Them Disappear

1. Being left by someone you love.

You're scared to commit because you think everyone will eventually leave you, but what you need to realize is that the right person chooses to stay. The right person won't wander when life becomes difficult, the right person will ask what they can do to make it easier. The right person makes you feel loved. They make you feel certain. They erase your fear of being left because they continue to prove that they will not only stay, but that they want to.

2. Uncertainty that they are right for you.

It's nearly impossible to know whether or not you're with the *right* person, but when it feels wrong, you'll know. Sometimes there's more than one person that is right for us, and sometimes we have to meet all the wrong people before finding them. Being uncertain about someone else is a reflection of the uncertainty you have within yourself. They say you need to love yourself before you can love someone else, but the same goes for trust. Trust yourself. Trust that you are smart enough to leave someone who doesn't show you the love that you deserve. It's okay to question. It's okay to be uncertain, but if you push everyone away, you're not only pushing away those who are completely wrong for you, you're pushing away everyone who's right.

3. Loss of independence.

When you commit to someone else, it's important to make the time to commit to yourself as well. You shouldn't have to compromise your independence to be with someone. A relationship involves two people. You are a couple, but you're not one item. You're not two halves that make one whole, you are two separate beings. You both have different passions, different hopes and dreams, and it is love that allows you to share them with one another. It is possible to share your life without giving up half of it.

4. Overwhelming feelings.

It's easy to care about family and friends more than ourselves, but when it comes to a relationship fear sets in deep. It's scary to care about someone so deeply that you question what you'd do without them, but you don't have to fear your feelings. It's okay to care, and more importantly it's okay to express how much you do, without the fear of pushing them away.

5. Having to put someone else first.

When you're single no one else's needs come before your own. If you want to go out, you go out. If you want to eat ice cream for dinner, you eat ice cream for dinner. There's no one there to tell you no, and there's no one else you need to satisfy. The only person you need to satisfy is yourself. Commitment is learning how to balance the two. Putting someone else's needs before your own only becomes a problem when you compromise your own happiness in the process. Do what you need to do to make you and your partner happy *together*. It's okay to put them first occasionally as long as you remember to maintain your own well-being while doing so.

6. Wondering if you're settling.

You're afraid to commit to one person because you wonder if you'll find someone better, but when you're with the right person, they'll be the *only* person you want to be with. You will come across people who are prettier, funnier, smarter; you will come across people who are 'better,' but they're not better for you. When you're with the right person, you won't want to give up what you have for someone else, no matter how attractive, cute or clever they may be. The right person, and the happiness you experience with them, outweighs all other indulgences you might desire.

7. Going through another terrible breakup.

Don't carry the failures of your last relationship into your present one, and don't let your scarring breakup, be a foreshadow of your future. Just because one of your relationships ended terribly doesn't mean they all have to. Learn from your past. Look back on the moments that hurt you and use them as ways to learn about yourself. If you fear commitment simply because you fear it ending you'll never be able to start a new beginning.

25

8 Real Ways To Allow Someone To Love You

1. Let them see you at your worst.

Because you can't always be at your best. They'll appreciate your vulnerability, and your willingness to be exactly who you are. If there's something you're trying to hide they'll attempt to discover what that is, and when you use distance in efforts to never let them see it, they'll feel unwanted. You want love in your life, so let others feel that you do.

2. Accept their help when needed.

No matter how super-human you can be, you're not invincible and occasionally it's okay to need a helping hand. Someone who loves you will want to help you, and when you don't let them you push them away.

3. Accept their compliments.

When they tell you that you're beautiful, don't disagree and self-deprecate, believe them. Trust that they wouldn't say it if they didn't mean it. They love you, but refuting their compliments will make them think that you don't love yourself.

4. Share your secrets.

But keep some too. Your connection becomes deeper when you let them in, but you don't have to use your personal skeletons as an attempt to make them stay. They will feel closer to you when you share something you haven't shared with others, but there's a difference between sharing something that it's important to you, and using secrets as strategy.

5. Let them meet the other loves of your life.

They have something in common with the other loves of your life and that is that they all love *you*. When someone matters to you, introduce them to everyone else who does too. You shouldn't have to keep your relationships separate. Someone you love should be integrated to all parts of your life.

6. Trust them.

Trust their words especially when they're attached to actions. Trust is something you can build together, but it's also something you can destroy individually. If you're questioning how they feel about you, or don't believe in their fidelity, it might be that you're trying to let the wrong person love you.

7. Let them do nice things for you.

They want to make you happy, so allow them to. Don't question their motives, just accept and enjoy that someone is willing to give you the love that you deserve, because you *do* deserve love.

8. Don't fear their abandonment.

If you're constantly afraid that they will leave you, you won't be able to enjoy the fact that they don't intend or want to. Embrace their commitment, accept that someone will want to love you without leaving you.

26

When You Change Your Life For Love And Hope It's All Worth It

Sometimes we compromise our wants and needs to maintain the love we have for someone else, and sometimes it works out, but other times it doesn't. And you won't know if it's truly worth it until you try, until you fall backwards hoping this person will be behind you, waiting with two feet sturdy on the ground and arms ready to break your fall, to catch you so you don't fall at all.

The skeptical part of you, the part of you that's realistic and sees things for what they are, feels like you're falling into nothing, falling *for* nothing, like you're jumping off an edge hoping you can fly.

And another part of you, the part that is hopeful and blissfully optimistic, the part that blindly walks into a room in hopes that your other senses won't fail you, thinks that you're doing the right thing. This part of you believes that everything *will* work out. That the sacrifices you are making will all be worth it.

And then all the other parts of you are blatantly lost. These parts of you are wandering in every direction, *pulling* you in every direction, leaving you uncertain of which one to take, which way to go.

And now you're torn. Torn between giving up the things that are important to you because it means you'll continue to be with the person who makes you happy, the person who means everything to you, the person who adds color to the blank canvas your life used to be without them, or to live life for yourself, *by* yourself, to live life the way you want to live it with no compromises, no sacrifice.

Because you're giving something up for someone else, *to be with* someone else. You're changing your life for them.

You need to decide how important this person is to you, if this relationship matters more than the things you're giving up to be with them. You need to consider what you'd do for them, and if they'd do the same in return. You need to think about what your life will be like *together*, and what it would mean if your lives were spent apart.

Because before you take this chance, before you make any decisions, you won't know whether or not they're *worth it*, you can't see into the future, see the way your lives will pan out together.

You can only choose to choose each other. You can choose to take chances. To make compromises and sacrifices, to live life not always for yourself, but to share it with someone else, to love, and to love big.

27

I Don't Need You To Say, "I Love You," I Need You To Show Me

Words can be spoken and promises made, but feelings and emotions are a language of their own. If you say you believe in us, how will I know it's true unless you show me?

Because it isn't difficult to *say* I love you, it's difficult to *prove* it. The challenge is the effort, not the declaration. And so many girls live for the day when someone professes their undying love, but I'd rather see it than hear it.

I don't wait for the day when you whisper in my ear that I mean everything to you, I wait for the day when I actually feel like I do.

Your words don't give me reassurance, and they shouldn't have to. I don't want to be reassured that your love is real, I want to *know* that it is. That's the beauty of knowing without it even being said.

Because I'd rather suffer through never hearing those words spoken, than suffer hearing them and feeling empty anyway.

It's how you make me feel that really matters. Because *anyone* can tell me that they love me, but you're the only one who can make me feel the way I do when I'm with you. And sometimes it's more comfortable to not say anything at all. Whether it is out of fear or complacency, our comfort shouldn't have to come from words alone. Because as good as words can feel, they can cause that much pain in return. And maybe we're not saying it because we're protecting ourselves from that same pain.

Because we each have a heart to keep guarded, and saying "I love you," will bring those walls down. And if we never say it, we never have to endure the agony of taking it back.

But there will be times when never saying it hurts even more, because if anyone should leave, you *feel* the love is gone, but you never had any confirmation that it was ever even there. Because when you show me that you love me it hurts that much more when you stop.

<u>28</u>

9 Things We Fear About Love That We Really Don't Need To

1. Being left.

We're scared of being left because we're scared to be alone, but the time you spend alone is something worth cherishing because instead of endlessly attempting to learn about someone else, you finally have the time to learn about yourself, and for some people that's terrifying. But a big part of love is learning that we have no control over who walks in or out of our lives, we only have control over what happens when they do. So even if they leave you, your ability to find love within yourself will allow you to share it with someone who not only deserves it, but never takes it for granted.

2. Letting someone in.

If you never let them in, they'll only see you from a distance. They will hear your words, but they won't feel them. They will see your actions, but they won't know the meaning behind them. And life might seem easier this way, because if you don't give someone parts of yourself that only you're familiar with, you don't give them the opportunity to walk away and leave you with less than what you started. You won't give them the opportunity to judge your insecurities, but their judgement isn't something you should be afraid of because chances are you're being harder on yourself than they would ever be.

3. Honesty.

How are you supposed to know when 'I love you' means more than a simple salutation? And how are you supposed to know when words are *meant* rather than just *said*? We can't foresee whether 'I'll love you forever,' will last as long as promised, but we can trust that real love wouldn't lie or deceive, and real love can make mistakes and most certainly will, but if you're as honest with yourself as you are with those you love, you'll understand that honesty isn't necessarily keeping a promise, it's accepting when you know a promise will be broken, and openly communicating why.

4. Wasting time with someone who's 'wrong' for you.

Time is one thing we fear with love because we look at the days, months, years, or decades spent with someone whose love didn't last as long as planned, and we wish we could have that time back so that we could spend it with someone whose love does last. And then we can't help but wonder how long it will take to find someone else who will somehow love us in return, but we think in terms of timing that doesn't necessarily make sense. It doesn't matter if you're 27 or 77, the time you spend sharing your heart and your life with someone isn't a waste simply because of an undesired outcome, it's a waste if you're too afraid to ever share your life at all.

5. Letting go.

Sometimes we hang onto people we know we shouldn't. Sometimes it's because we can't let go. Sometimes it's because we choose not to. And sometimes we confuse the difference between the two. You're not *incapable* of letting go, you simply fear what might happen if you do. You're holding onto something that isn't working, in hopes that maybe it will, but eventually your own happiness will outweigh the fear of being alone.

6. Moving on.

Once you get over the fear of letting go, you have to face the fear of moving on. As hard as it is to get over something that's been lost, it's equally as hard to have the courage to find something even better. One part of you thinks you never will, another part of you tries to tell yourself that's okay, and the smallest part of you still hopes that you'll find love again.

7. Second chances.

We're scared to give second chances because the pain we already felt, could possibly hurt us all over again, and we survived the first time, but we're scared we won't survive the second. And then there's not knowing whether the second chance will be worth it, whether the changes you both have gone through have not only made you ready to try again, but have made you both more compatible than you were before. And no matter what the other person does, says, or feels, you're the only person who can convince yourself whether or not the second chance is worth taking.

8. Losing the spark.

It's not always the loss of love we're most afraid of, but the loss of lust, of absolute infatuation, and the bliss of the beginning. Because once we lose the spark, we become bored, and when we become bored we look for something else, and when that something else begins to fill the space where sparks no longer exist, we forget what caused the sparks to ignite in the first place. But if we remember that the spark is something we created, then we can learn how to make it happen again.

9. Someone won't accept your flaws, and will leave when they discover them.

We're scared to let others see our imperfections only because we're scared we won't live up to their expectations, but love isn't about making sure every expectation has been met, it's about learning how to adapt when they're not. Perfection doesn't have to be your aspiration, aspire to find someone who understands that 'perfect' is something you'll never be.

<u>29</u>

This Is What Will Happen If You Take Her Love For Granted

If you take her love for granted, she'll take the first step towards walking away.

You'll think she's becoming distant, but you won't do enough in efforts to make her stay. And then her first step will lead to a second and her second to a third, and before you know it she'll have walked out of your life completely and you'll wonder what you did to make her leave, because in your eyes you did nothing at all, but that's exactly it. She left because of what you *didn't* do, she left because she was smart enough, brave enough, to realize that she deserved better.

Because you weren't her only option. She chose to love you for as long as you were willing to love her in return, and when you took the love she chose to give you for granted, she was unafraid to leave it all behind, even if it meant that she had to be alone. Because it wasn't so much the loneliness that scared her, it was the fact that the love she had given you for all this time was wasted, because even though she proved to herself she was capable of loving someone, you didn't prove to her that her love was worth it.

Because she showed you love in little moments that you thought weren't big enough to mean something. But for her the little moments meant everything. It was the little moments that showed how much she cared.

She showed love like good morning kisses and little notes left on the fridge to make you smile. She showed love like covering you with blankets when you fell asleep on the couch and setting her alarm because she knew you'd forget to set yours. She showed love like holding your hand on train rides home because even though you were right next to her, she wanted the comfort of your touch. She showed love like goodnight texts on weekends spent without you, to let you know that even though she was dancing carelessly with friends, she was thinking of you.

She showed love in ways you took for granted, ways you only appreciated after she was gone.

And it wasn't a matter of making her feel wanted, because she didn't need validation through your desire. She knew you still wanted her, still loved her, and cared, but she also knew that even if it was never your intention to lose her, or push her away, she could no longer be with someone who made her feel like the love she had to give was incomplete.

If you take her love for granted, you'll regret the love you were too oblivious to see, the love you were too oblivious to feel, to respond to. If you take her love for granted, hope that you'll realize it before she's gone.

If you take her love for granted, and in return she leaves, you'll continuously wish you could go back. And if she's the kind of girl who believes in second chances, you might have the opportunity to make her happy she gave you one. But if she's the kind of girl who doesn't look for love in a place where it's already been lost, she will find love somewhere else. She will find love with someone who appreciates it from beginning to end.

30

This Is How You Make Her Stay

Make her stay by sharing your life with her, and not just the good parts, but the parts you're scared for her to see. Let her beneath the surface you keep guarded because that's where you two will grow together, and that's the only type of depth that will lessen the distance between you.

Make her stay by letting her protect you. She doesn't need you to always be strong; she sees humility in your weakness. Don't fear her judgement, she wants to help you, not hurt you. Know that she is more accepting than you realize.

Make her stay by showing her she matters. She doesn't look to you to feel significant, but when you take her kindness for granted, she notices, and not only does she notice, she absorbs. And if she absorbs the fact that she is unimportant she will either try that much harder, or shut herself off from you completely. And you'll question what is wrong, but she won't tell you because she'll think she's simply over-reacting. But if you give her the love that she deserves, there's no reason for her to doubt or drift, there's only reason for her to be sure that she's exactly where she's supposed to be.

Make her stay by telling her how you really feel. And don't just say it, show it. Don't pretend to be indifferent if she's the best thing that's ever happened to you. Let her know, because it's just as painful to regret the things you never said than it is to say them and be disappointed with her reaction. Every expectation makes room for let down. Don't expect, don't predict, don't worry, just be, and be authentically yourself.

Make her stay by giving her reason to trust you. Because trust ventures far beyond fidelity. Trust gives her the confidence to let you in, and once she lets you in, she's not going anywhere.

Make her stay by being present. Be the person who's there when life couldn't be better, and don't disappear when it gets worse. Make her feel as though you're there to stay, so that she doesn't have to worry about who will leave first.

31

She Was Afraid She'd Break His Heart Because She Was Still Putting Hers Back Together

She looked at him and knew he'd never hurt her, knew he'd never leave her unexpectedly, or break her heart like it had been broken before. And although she was completely secure in the way he felt about her, the way he looked at her and couldn't help but smile, the way he consistently made her feel loved, the way he made her feel that he was there to stay, she began to see all of these things that he gave so easily to her, and wondered what it was she was giving to him in return.

She began to doubt the love she had to give because of the love that she was shown, because he showed her love that was *more* than enough, love that was strong and certain, love that was authentic and real. He showed her *remarkable* love, and that's the kind of love she'd never been shown. And this remarkable love is everything she was afraid of. She was afraid of finding someone who trusted her with their heart, someone who put his heart in her hands and expected her to hold it.

Because she was so used to being the one to give her heart away, she was used to being the one who was scared of being hurt. And now that she finally found someone who she knew would never hurt her, she was scared of the fact that she could possibly hurt him. **She was afraid to break his heart because hers was still being put back together.**

And she wasn't sure if her heart would ever truly be whole, because the last time it was broken she realized her heart isn't something that needs to be fixed, because each time someone would hurt or disappoint her, she left a little part of herself behind. She left a part of her heart with the people who hurt it. But she realized that's okay.

It's okay to scatter pieces of your heart with temporary people, temporary places, temporary things and circumstances, because the more places your heart has been scattered the more love you've proven you can give. And now he was leaving a part of his heart with her, a part that she hadn't yet damaged, a part that he knew she would keep, and she would. Because even if she did hurt him, even if she dropped the heart he trusted her to hold, she knew the love they'd leave behind would still be remarkable.

And every time he said the words, "I love you," she'd say it back with no questions asked, no chord of doubt or waver in her voice, because she knew that she loved him, and she knew that her love was dependable, but whether or not someone would get hurt along the way was something she'd never truly know.

She knows when it comes to love 'hurt' is something that's never intended, and heartbreak is something she'll continue to be afraid of, for both herself and for him, but the fact that she's afraid to break his heart shows just how hard she'll try to never let it happen.

32

Love The Girl Whose Happiness Does Not Depend On You

She doesn't *need* you to be happy, but you're likely one of the biggest reasons why she is.

She's happy when she's with you, when you make her smile out of stupidity, when you kiss her cheek just because you can, when you ask her if she's okay, and when you try to make her feel better because you know that she's not. She's happy when you look at her like something you've never seen before, when you tell her that she's beautiful, and when she rolls her eyes in reply. She's happy when you grab her for no reason and tell her that you love her, simply because you feel it so much that you have to let her know. She's happy when you're around.

These are the moments where happiness lives, where the two of you are happy together. Because when you two are together happiness is something that exists *between* you, it's not one-sided or dependent, it is *shared*. It just happens, and you both experience that same feeling.

And while the happiness shared between you, between your bodies, your minds, your spirit and your soul, is so breathtakingly beautiful, you both have the ability to be happy when the other's not around. You both understand that the happiness you experience with this person is one of the better places you can find it, but it's certainly not the *only* place.

And in a way that's what makes your love so strong. The fact that you can be happy with *and* without each other. The fact that you've found happiness within and outside of yourselves. Because while other people can make you happy, they can also disappoint you, but if you remember the things that you enjoy purely because *you* enjoy them, your happiness will live forever.

It will grow and change and sometimes you'll think it has disappeared, but when you find the right person to share it with, they'll remind you it's still there. They'll remind you what happiness feels like, and you'll realize you've had the ability to feel it all along.

Because you're the girl who can find happiness within herself. You're the girl whose happiness does not *depend* on others, but is *shared* with others.

33

Love The Person You Can Have Fun Doing Absolutely Nothing With

He put his feet up on her coffee table and rested his head on her shoulder. It didn't matter what was on the TV, it didn't matter whether she was drinking herbal tea or wine, it didn't matter that she was wearing an old stained t-shirt with sweats, none of that mattered, because when she was with him they could be doing nothing at all. It was the reassurance of his touch, the comfort in her laugh, the happiness felt in the presence of the other.

It was the love they felt simply by sharing their lives together, no matter what they were doing.

Their love grew in adventure, in doing things that were exciting, things that guaranteed smiles, laughter, things that automatically caused conversation. But those moments weren't the ones where they discovered how much they meant to each other, how much they loved one another, and how much they'd change their lives for the sake of loving someone else.

Because while their love *grew* in moments of excitement, moments of thrill and spiked heartbeats, it *thrived* in moments of quiet, in moments of calm and silence,

moments of nothingness. Moments that weren't memorable at all, but moments that most certainly maintained the love that already existed. Because they didn't need adrenaline or thrill to enjoy each other's company. They had fun together while doing nothing at all. They loved each other in every moment, not just the exhilarating ones.

And as time went on, and the excitement of simply being with one another was *supposed to wear down*, when their love was *supposed to* become complacent, not weaker, but just different, they discovered that their love was more resilient than they'd ever imagine.

Because although she knew she loved him in drunken nights on dance floors and weekend getaways where they escaped reality together, she also knew she loved him after long days of work that ended in the comfort of his arms, she knew she loved him in lazy Sunday mornings of cooking breakfast and staying in pajamas all day, she knew she loved him when the moments that were *supposed* to be boring were better when spent with him.

Love someone who brings joy to the moments that are *supposed* to be boring. Love someone who doesn't have to always make you smile, but supplements your happiness regardless of visible grins or audible laughter. Because while life might not always be exciting, it is better when they're around. Love the person you have fun doing absolutely nothing with.

34

I Want Every Day With You To Feel Like The First

The beginning phase is always the best, and apparently we're in it, and if what *they* say is true this feeling will run out, but I don't want to think about the day when I wake up not feeling the way I do right now with you.

I want every day with you to feel like the first.

I want it to feel like the beginning, because even if we're far from day one we should still remember how to love each other, how to make one another feel special, and wanted.

I don't want the butterflies to be replaced with exhaustion, or annoyance, or spite. I want the butterflies to stay. I still want the same smile to unconsciously appear when I look at my phone and see your name, the smile that happens unintentionally, the smile that happens when everyone around me knows I'm thinking of you.

I still want to feel like I never want you to leave, and I still want to feel an unnecessary loneliness when you do. Because

I know I'll be seeing you again soon, but I still want it to feel like it's never soon enough.

I still want there to be effort. I still want the happiness to be maintained, and for each of us to continue to do the little things that show how much we care. I still want to show you that you matter, to show you that even if there's a time in my life when other things come before you, you still have a place here.

I still want the laughter to be exhilarating.

I still want *your* laugh to make *me* laugh, and I still want to think, 'Wow, I love him' when it does.

I still want you to be the first thing I think about when I wake up. I still want *you* to think of *me*.

I still want to unknowingly bring you up in daily conversations, to talk about how wonderful you are without even realizing it.

I still want you to give me a reason to feel lucky, to feel lucky that someone like you would love someone like me. Someone who makes love feel certain, someone who makes *me* feel certain.

I still want that nervousness, the same nervousness I felt when you first whispered that you loved me. When I admitted I was scared, and you reassured me that I didn't have to be.

I want the feeling of beginning to endure until the end.

I want to make you feel like every day with me is the first, and I want to make you feel like you'll never have to worry about there being a last.

About the Author

Nicole is a Writer/Producer for Thought Catalog. She has a passion for writing (obviously) and loves to read anything based on a true story.

Check out more of her writing on Thought Catalog at thoughtcatalog.com/nicole-tarkoff and follow her on Twitter @tarkofftarkon!

Thought Catalog, it's a website.
www.thoughtcatalog.com

Social
facebook.com/thoughtcatalog
twitter.com/thoughtcatalog
tumblr.com/thoughtcatalog
instagram.com/thoughtcatalog

Corporate
www.thought.is

Made in the USA
Middletown, DE
12 February 2021